Percy Aldridge GRAINGER

FIVE FOLKSONGS AND A FROCK COAT

Arranged by
Richard W. Sargeant, Jr.

Study Score
Partitur

SERENISSIMA MUSIC, INC.

CONTENTS

1. Country Gardens, BFMS 22 3
2. Spoon River, AFMS 1 11
3. Molly on the Shore, BFMS 1 21
4. Irish Tune from County Derry, BFMS 6 40
5. Handel in the Strand, RMTB 1 44
6. Shepherd's Hey, BFMS 3 54

ENSEMBLE

2 oboes, 2 clarinets
2 horns, 2 bassoons

Duration: ca. 17 minutes

ISBN: 978-1-60874-086-4

Printed in the USA
First Printing: February, 2013

FIVE FOLKSONGS and a FROCK COAT
1. Country Gardens

Percy Aldridge Grainger
arr. by Richard W. Sargeant, Jr.

Copyright © Serenissima Music, Inc.
All rights reserved.   Printed in USA

8

2. Spoon River

Sturdily, not too fast; with "pioneer" persistency. ♩ = 168

3. Molly on the Shore

30

34

4. Irish Tune From County Derry

Slowish, but not dragged, and wayward in time. ♪ = between 72 and 104
(Rubato il tempo, e non troppo lento)

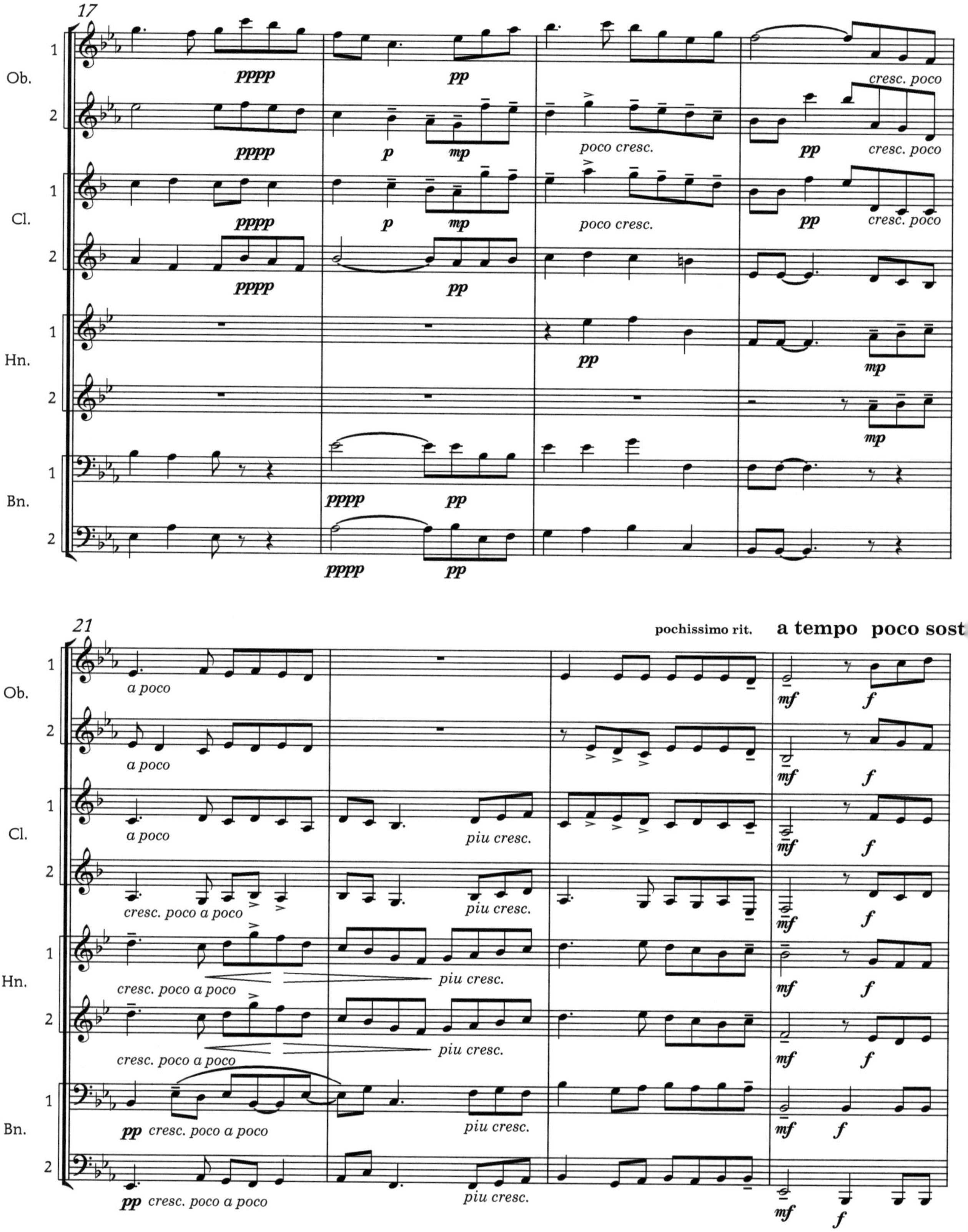
17
Ob.
Cl.
Hn.
Bn.
pppp
pp
p
mp
poco cresc.
cresc. poco
21
pochissimo rit.
a tempo poco sost
a poco
cresc. poco a poco
piu cresc.
mf
f

5. Handel in the Strand

Fast & Merry, Very rigid in time. ♩ = 120 -132

46

6. Shepherd's Hey

Printed by Libri Plureos GmbH in Hamburg, Germany